Dog & Puppy Training Box Set

Dog Training
The Complete Dog Training Guide For A Happy, Obedient, Well Trained Dog

+

Puppy Training
The Complete Guide To Housebreak Your Puppy in Just 7 Days

Dan O'Brian

©Copyright 2015 by Dan O'Brian - All rights reserved.

This document is geared towards providing exact and reliable information in regards to the topic and issue covered. The publication is sold with the idea that the publisher is not required to render accounting, officially permitted, or otherwise, qualified services. If advice is necessary, legal or professional, a practiced individual in the profession should be ordered.

- From a Declaration of Principles which was accepted and approved equally by a Committee of the American Bar Association and a Committee of Publishers and Associations.

In no way is it legal to reproduce, duplicate, or transmit any part of this document in either electronic means or in printed format. Recording of this publication is strictly prohibited and any storage of this document is not allowed unless with written permission from the publisher. All rights reserved.

The information provided herein is stated to be truthful and consistent, in that any liability, in terms of inattention or otherwise, by any usage or abuse of any policies, processes, or directions contained within is the solitary and utter responsibility of the recipient reader. Under no circumstances will any legal responsibility or blame be held against the publisher for any reparation, damages, or monetary loss due to the information herein, either directly or indirectly.

Respective authors own all copyrights not held by the publisher.

The information herein is offered for informational purposes solely, and is universal as so. The presentation of the information is without contract or any type of guarantee assurance.

The trademarks that are used are without any consent, and the publication of the trademark is without permission or backing by the trademark owner. All trademarks and brands within this book are for clarifying purposes only and are the owned by the owners themselves, not affiliated with this document.

Dog Training

The Complete Dog Training Guide For A Happy, Obedient, Well Trained Dog

Table of Contents

Introduction vii

Chapter 1: Where to Start After Deciding You Want a Dog 1

Chapter 2: Training Your New Dog 9

Chapter 3: How To House Train Your New Dog 13

Chapter 4: Basic Obedience Training 19

Chapter 5: Advanced Dog Training Commands 27

Chapter 6: Socialization Skills 41

Chapter 7: Training Dos and Don'ts 43

Conclusion 49

Introduction

I want to thank you and congratulate you for purchasing the book, *"Dog Training: The complete dog training guide for a happy, obedient, well trained dog"*.

This book has comprehensive information on how to train your dog.

Having a dog can be one of the greatest things that anyone can ever have. There is a reason why many say that a dog is man's best friend. But just because you got a dog does not automatically mean that you will be the best of friends and have the best of a dog-owner relationship. In fact, if you don't do something to mold your dog the way you want it to be, having a dog can be one of the most frustrating and annoying things you could ever have.

For instance, if you don't train the dog, it might be the kind that never gets off the couch, the kind that poops or pees anywhere and everywhere, the kind that jumps on guests, the kind that cries immediately you put it in the crate, or the kind that you simply cannot fathom going to different places like shopping with. Well, I wouldn't consider that a friend.

Many frustrated dog owners started with the best of intentions hoping that they would have the cute little dog that would accompany them wherever they go without causing ugly scenes like barking at strangers or threatening other dogs. If you have a dog that has some of the annoying habits that you wish it could change so that you can live the life that you've always wanted with your dog, then you need to train the dog to mold its behavior.

There is nothing special about those German shepherds that you see performing some drills that you never thought a dog would do. It all depends on how you train the dog. If you want to transform your dog with proper training, this book will help you to do just that. It will teach you everything you need to do to transform your unruly dog to one that you always adore thanks to its ability to do anything that you want.

Thanks again for purchasing this book, I hope you enjoy it!

Just as there are many dog breeds, dog training is just as varied. Unfortunately, many people think that dog training is something done to a dog to make it execute some artificial command. Dog training has much to do with training your dog to be obedient: to obey everything and anything that comes close to him.

Dog training covers a wide range of lessons, which include training your dog new tricks, family manners and many dog skills. Contrary to popular belief, every dog can be trained to a professional level. People assume that training sniffing dogs, service dogs meant for handicapped owners, rescue and search dogs, hunting, carting and sled dogs is a reserve of professional dog trainers. That is not so. In fact, the most highly trained dogs you know are simply carrying out their obedience training to the highest degree. They are trained to behave according to a set of commands that boost their value as helpers to their owner. After training your dog, it will be much more of a pet other than just a wild card. So how do you get started?

CHAPTER 1

Where to Start After Deciding You Want a Dog

Owning a happy, obedient, and well-trained dog is an amazing experience. However, training a dog takes a lot of work and getting started is never easy especially if you have never owned a dog before. Training a dog or puppy takes a ton of work and preparation and with a few unplanned for surprises along the way.

While this may be so, it helps to have some guidance so you can know where to begin when you have made the life changing decision to own a dog. Once you make the decision to buy or adopt a dog or puppy, there are fundamental things you must do to raise and train a happy dog. Below are tips to help you start on the right track as you embark on this fulfilling journey: the journey of being a well-trained dog owner.

1: List Things You Need For Your Dog

Making a list is the best way to break down any difficult task to make it manageable. Likewise, this would be the best way to get started when you have decided to own a dog.

Make a list of the things you will need before your dog comes home, i.e. all the things you need immediately after, and within the first six months of taking your dog home. Doing this will allow you to figure out how much time and money you will need to budget for your dog.

Although you can approach preparation in different ways, here are a few pointers.

Before

Crate; choose a crate that is durable and comfortable. Since crates come in a variety of materials, i.e. fiberglass, wire and heavy molded plastic crate, ask your trainer or veterinarian to recommend to you the best type of crate suitable for your dog.

Note: Some wire crates collapse from easy movements around the house, while molded plastic crates tend to be great for airplane travel in case your dog travels in the cargo bay.

Your crate should be big enough to allow your dog stretching space, as well as turn around and get comfortable space. However, your crate should not be too big. Choose a crate that is fitting for your dog in his or her full-grown size.

Beddings: Choose an easy to clean bedding that is thick enough for comfort.

Water and food bowls: Use ceramic or stainless steel and paint free bowls. Avoid using plastic bowls since they absorbs bacteria and smells.

Flea comb: A flea comb is used as a flea control mechanism.

Brush: Brush your dog on daily basis. It is good for skin and better than bathing.

Pet cleaners: Examples of pet cleaners are; simple solution or nature miracle. They are available in pet supply stores. They remove pet stains and odors.

After

As soon as your dog comes home, it will need an initial check up at the vet's office, tick and flea prevention, and pet insurance if necessary.

If you are a novice, you will need to schedule dog training and obedience classes.

Within the first 6 months of your dog's life, you will need at most three rounds of shots over the first few days and a neuter or a spay appointment.

2: Choosing a Dog

Choosing a dog is more of a compromise than an art. Nevertheless, as a dog owner, you should have a preference beforehand. For instance, do you want a high-energy running dog? Or do you want a small and quiet dog since you live in an apartment? Well, the following are the things you need to consider while choosing what you want in your dog.

The Age You Want Your Dog To Be When Coming Home; by adopting an older dog, you can be able to skip crate and house training, whereas a young puppy will need some training, which will have a greater impact on how your dog's behavior is molded and shaped.

The Size of The Dog You Want: the bigger the dog, the more it eats and the more space it needs. Some people like big dogs especially if they're living alone and want to feel protected.

Are You Ready To Train Your Dog? If yes, you need to consider the breeds of dogs that are easier to train. Some breeds are difficult to train than others. Some of the easy to train breeds include Labrador Retriever, Australian Shepherd, Belgian Sheepdog, Poodles, Golden Retriever, Australian Cattle Dog, Border Collie, German Shepherd, Doberman Pinscher and Bloodhounds.

3: Figure out Which Breeds Fit Your Lifestyle

Every dog breed has its own popular characteristics, starting from high energy to being tough to train. Therefore, you need to spend some time doing research on different dog characteristics in relation to breeds. You can use sources such as Animal Planet Dog Breeder selection or American Kennel Club to gain some insight into your preferred dog characteristics.

Animal Plant Dog Breeder - http://www.animalplanet.com/dog-breed-selector/

American Kennel Club - http://www.akc.org/

Sometimes, you may get overwhelmed by a dog breed you barely know. Research will help you get the most out of it and make sure you approach choosing a dog from a knowledgeable point about what you might be looking for in terms of personality.

4: Where to Find Your Dog; Breeder vs. Shelter

While opinions are divided between choosing a dog from a breeder or shelter, you will find that one of them is the best for you. However, the truth is that at the end of it, a lot has to do with the individual than it does with the dog. The decision to choose from a breeder or a shelter is often a heavy one for most new dog owners.

Breeder-With breeders, you will find it much easier to control the outcome, which tends to be great for the novice dog owners or the experienced dog owners who has particular needs and preferences.

Dogs found in breeders come home with only the first round of vaccination but they have fewer cases of dog abuse or troubled pasts. If you opt to go with the breeder option, it is highly recommended that you buy your dog from a responsible dog breeder such as a Kennel Club.

Kennel Club - http://www.akc.org/dog-breeders/

Shelter-shelter dogs are wildcards. In many cases, you will not know more about a sheltered dog's past in terms of abuse or neglect the dog may have suffered before.

If you have researched the kind of breed you want and are not sure of the breed to go for, or feel the need to check out the various breeds from somewhere else other than internet, a shelter is an ideal place.

Sheltered dogs are likely to be vaccinated, spayed, and sometime micro chipped.

5: Picking Up Your Dog

When picking up your dog, try to find out the kind of diet the dog eats to avoid stomach problems. Stick to that meal plan for the first few days. In case you want to switch to a different type of food, do it over a period of one week by adding one portion of new food to three portions of the previous meals.

In rare cases, some dogs find car trips stressful. In this case, secure your dog in a crate to make the journey a bit easier and safer. Immediately after bringing your dog home, take them to the toilet area of the house, and spend some time with them there to get the dog accustomed to that area and use it to relieve themselves.

Next, place your dog on a leash and walk it around the house. Since your dog might be anxious about this new place, don't be surprised if the dog exhibits insistent pacing and panting, excessive drinking, house training accidents and chewing or gastric upset. A male dog that was not neutered early might mark the new territory especially if you have other pets living there. Give your dog enough space to settle down to avoid your new dog being overwhelmed.

Next, take your dog to its crate. Take your time to encourage your dog to sniff around, and reward him with small treats for entering the crate. Put some soft beddings and safe toys in the crate and leave him to relax.

6: Naming Your Dog

Naming your dog is the first step towards developing a close bond between you and your dog. However, coming up with a companion's names may be harder than you think. Below are tips to help you pick your dog's name.

Keep It Short, Crisp and Sweet

While naming your dog, limit its name to one or two syllables, just to make sure that your dog can easily understand it. Long dog names will only confuse your dog, since lengthy names are incomprehensible to the canine due to their long weird sounding wordings and intonations.

Try Out Names with Sharp Consonants

Dogs are good at hearing sounds with high frequency; names starting with s, ch, sh, etc., are good at catching a dog's attention. These sharp names will enable your dog to respond quickly compared to other names. Further, consider names that end with long vowels; this can be a short "a" or a long "e" sound, i.e. Kassie, sweetie, samba, Charlie, or Delilah.

Never mix dog commands like "down", "sit", "come", with the name of your dog. This causes confusion and your dog might not respond correctly. For instance, "bit", and "sit", or "fay" and "stay"

Stick to Similar Sounds While Renaming an Older Dog

Be cautious when you want to change an older dog's name. Stick to a similar name as the previous one. For example, changing "barney" to "Farley", it's crucial to maintain the vowel sounds similar than the consonants, because dogs pick up vowel easily and that what he listens to. i.e. "pinky" will go along with "Mikey" but not "Pokey".

CHAPTER 2

Training Your New Dog

Every dog should be trained. Your dog should know basic manners, important things and a few tricks. After you bring your new dog home, you will be ready to start training. To maximize your dog's learning potential and ensure you are both enjoying the training classes, keep the following tips in mind.

Training Tips for New Dog Owners

Keep Training Sessions Sweet And Short: whenever you are teaching your dog new skills, it tends to be like a young child. Dogs do not have long attention spans. While there is no hard and fast rule in dog training, an ideal dog training session should not exceed 15 minutes.

During a single session, you can choose to introduce one new skill or switch between a few different skills. To keep your training interesting, try to do 5-15 repetitions of similar behavior followed by 5-15 repetitions of another behavior.

You can also introduce new skills to your dog and improve the old ones by doing single repetitions at suitable times during the day. For instance, before serving your dog meals, ask him to sit or lie down first.

Before the end of a training session, quit on a good note by ending it with a skill you know your dog is good at. This will ensure you have ended the session without either one of you getting bored, tired, or frustrated.

Note that dogs were not born with an understanding of English. They can only learn significant words such as, walk, sit, treat etc. If you combine these familiar words with complex sentences, your dog will get confused. For instance, you might confuse your dog by saying "fluffy down", then another day you say to your dog, "sit down" "fluffy". If you do this, you might wonder why fluffy does not act the same way every time. While teaching your dog a command or cue, choose just one phrase or word that you will consistently be using all through.

Take baby steps. Dogs are similar to us in many ways. For example, dogs learn better when new tasks are broken down. When introducing a new skill, start with easy steps and increase difficulty as you proceed. For instance, when you are training your dog to stay, begin with 3 seconds stay, then increase the stay to a duration of 8 seconds. After your dog has mastered the 8-second stay, make things a bit harder by increasing the time to 15secs, 30secs, etc. This will make your dog learn faster.

Work on one particular skill at a time. Most of the skills you want your dog to learn are complex. For example, if you want your dog to learn a solid sit-stay, you should teach him to stay in a sitting position until you release him. This can be; he should stay until you move from him or stay until things around distract him. If you teach your dog different skills at the same time, you and the dog might end up frustrated. Instead, start with one skill, and after mastering that skill, introduce another.

For instance, work on duration first. When he can stay-sit for a few minute in a quiet place that has no distractions, stand next to him, start training him as you move away from where he is. Focusing on that new skill, go back and ask him to sit for a while. Stay around and build up the duration of the stay again. Proceed by training him in a more distracting place. Gradually proceed by making the skills harder and harder but in an easier way. At the end of it, your dog will have mastered everything.

When you run into trouble, go back a few steps. If you introduce a new skill to your dog and fail to see any progress, you will have increased the level of its difficulty too quickly. In this case, refresh his memory by making a few repetitions. Start from the skill you know your dog can perform well and practice for a while without adding to the difficulty.

Practice the learnt skills everyone and with anyone. Dogs tend to learn very specifically and do not apply what they learnt in different situations, people, and places. If you teach your dog to stay in kitchen, he will be a kitchen-trained dog. However, ask him to sit at a different locations and he might not understand what you mean. For him to perform his skills everywhere, practice skills at different places; your yard and home, in the street, at a friend's place or at the park.

Use real rewards. Get used to rewarding your dog with things he finds truly rewarding. You will find that some dogs will happily train in your room and ignore the training while in the park. This might be because the park is very distracting which makes it hard for him to pay attention to the training sessions.

Pay your dog according to the reward that is worth working for. This can be bits of chicken or cheese, or a chance to run off-leash with his friends at the park. Note that the reward might change at a given time. If he has eaten his meal, a scratch behind his ears would be more rewarding than chicken and cheese. If he has not eaten for some time, then a reward based on bites would be worth.

Be persistent. Training your dog might take you some time and effort. Take it slow, and with time, you and your dog will accomplish great things.

CHAPTER 3

How To House Train Your New Dog

House training an adult dog or a puppy may appear daunting, but every dog can be trained how to eat, play, sleep, relieve himself outside and so on. It is up to you as a dog owner to teach your dog responsible behavior that go along with your requirements.

Note that punishing your dog has never been a remedy to bad behavior. Instead, punishment only scares away your dog. A good sense of humor and patience are the key to helping your dog adapt to life as a pet. Below are three easy ways to house train your new dog.

Setting up A Routine

The first thing to factor in while house training your new dog is coming up with a routine. Here is how it goes…

1: Take Your Dog Outside Frequently

Taking your dog outside time after time is one of the crucial things to do while teaching your dog to relieve himself. While it may appear to be excessive, take him outside as frequently as possible, about every half an hour. Stick to this schedule and try not to miss even one chosen "outside" time so as your dog can associate this outside time with relieving himself.

In case you are training a puppy, take him outside more frequently because puppies have small bladders and can't hold their pee for long.

2: Put Your Dog on a Feeding Schedule

Get into a routine of feeding your dog at the same time in the morning and at night. After the meals, wait 20-30 minutes before you take him outside. A feeding schedule will help you predict when your dog needs to go to the bathroom, hence making house training a bit effortless.

For a puppy, create a three-meals-per-day feeding schedule bearing in mind that he needs to be taken outside more frequently.

3: Learn To Interpret Signs That Your Dog Has To Go

These signs include; walking around stiffly, holding its tail in a funny position, sniffing the floor as if he is looking for something and so on. Once your dog shows the signs that he wants to pee or poop, take him outside immediately even if it's before the outside time.

Include verbal cues like saying "outside" before you take him out. Eventually, you will be in a position to ask him if he needs to go outside by saying the word.

4: Choose a Specific Spot Outside

Choose a specific place where you will be taking your dog each time you take him out. This can be somewhere in your backyard or close to a green patch of grass. Dogs are creatures of habit.

When he gets used to this spot, it will be his most comfortable place to pee each time he goes outside.

Once you reach the spot you have designated, use a verbal cue such as "go potty". This will help him associate relieving himself with the place.

5: Keep Your Dog In A Crate At Night And When You Are Away

If you leave your dog free to roam the house during the night, he might end up soiling the floor. To avoid this mess, keep him in a comfortable crate at night and when you are not around. Dogs dislike soiling their dens, so he will have to wait until he can go out to relieve himself.

Note that dogs should see their crates as their safe place and should enjoy spending time there. In this case, don't keep your dog in the crate as a form of punishing him. When you use it in that manner, he will associate the crate with fear instead of comfort.

Also, don't let your dog stay in the crate for too long before going outside. If he does, he will have no choice other than relieving himself in there. Your dog will need plenty of exercises, and play time, so he should be in the crate for no more than a few hours or overnight.

6: Clean Up Messes Immediately

If your dog makes a mess indoors, which tends to be normal, clean it up instantly and use a cleaning solution to get rid of the smell. In case your dog smells old mess at a particular spot, he will think of that place as a potty spot.

Don't punish your dog when they make a mess; simply clean it up and get back to the schedule.

Rewarding Your Dog For Good Behavior

Did you know that dogs need to be rewarded after every single time they stick to a particular good behavior? Yes! Your dog will do anything to get a reward! Take advantage of that by rewarding him anytime he does it right. Below are some of the cases you will need to reward your dog after setting up a routine…

1: Give Your Dog Praise and a Treat Every Time He Goes Outside Successfully

Your dog will learn best through positive reinforcement and he will quickly learn the best way of achieving it. Each time your dog uses his designated spot in the right way, reward him with lots of praises, a little treat and a scratch on the head.

You need to be consistent when it comes to rewarding your dog. Do it every time he goes to the potty in the potty spot and after learning all the other good behavior.

2: Time Rewards Correctly

When treating your dog for using his potty spot correctly, do it once he relieves himself. Don't do it too early or too late because he will not associate it with relieving himself in the right spot.

3: Consider Using a Chime or a Bell to Aid in Training

Some people attain dog-training success while using the bell method instead of a treat. After your dog relieves himself in the potty spot, ring a bell or a pleasant-sounding chime as a way of rewarding him. Your dog will look forward to the sound of the chime.

4: Keep Your Tone and Manner Light and Friendly

Each time you are taking your dog to the potty or talking about it, keep your voice pleasant and light. Do not raise your voice or talk in a harsh tone, because your dog can take his bodily functions as a punishment and associate it with fear. If he messes indoors, withhold the praise instead of yelling at him.

When you are using verbal cues like "go potty", "outside", or "good dog" be consistent. Repeat these words along with the environment and actions to reinforce where you want him to relieve himself.

Paper Training Your Dog in an Apartment

Were you worried whether you can still adopt a dog in an apartment? Well you can. Here is how to train your dog to be well mannered even when he is indoors most of the time.

1: Choose an Out-Of-The-Way Spot That Is Easy For Your Dog to Access

If your house is located in a high rise, it almost impossible to make it outside every time your dog wants to relieve himself.

Instead, pick a spot inside your house that is not right in the middle of your living room but also easy for your dog to access at any time. This can be a corner of the laundry room or kitchen. Let the spot be in a hard wood or vinyl flooring space instead of a carpet.

2: Line the Designated Spot with Training Pads or Newspapers

Newspaper is affordable material you can use while creating a potty for your dog. If you choose to use the absorbent training pads, you can find them in pet stores.

You can as well use a dog litter tray. In case you want your dog to adopt reliving himself outdoor and indoor, fill up the tray with soil for the dog to associate that as an acceptable area to relieve himself.

3: Change The Mat Often But Leave A Small Spot Of Dried Urine On There

As said earlier, old urine smell will remind your dog that the mat is the place to go potty. Get rid of feces right away but leave a small spot of paddling or newspaper with urine on the clean mat so your dog will know the place to go.

4: Reward Your Dog for Going in the Right Spot

Every time your dog relieves himself on the mat, reward him with petting, praise and a treat. He will associate going potty in the mat with the positive feeling, and eventually, he will start going there without help.

CHAPTER 4

Basic Obedience Training

Trying to control your dog before learning obedience commands is tiresome and almost impossible. However, teaching him 5 basic commands will make a world of difference and provide a great chance for bonding.

Note that puppies have short attention spans. It is unreasonable to expect your puppy's attention to last for long periods. In this case, keep your sessions short and increase the duration gradually.

The Sit Command

The sit command is one of the easiest skills to teach. A dog that sits on command is easier to manage before he learns more self-control. For instance, if you teach your dog to sit when the doorbell rings, there will be minimal chances of him jumping on visitors when the door opens.

How to teach sit

1. Get on the same level with your puppy, either on the floor or in a chair next to him.

2. Hold a treat next to his nose and let him follow the treat as you move your hand up.

3. While his head moves up, his butt will lower down.

4. After his butt hits the floor, place the treat in his mouth and instantly praise him for his intelligence and obedience.

5. Repeat this multiple times every day. Pair this behavior with the word "sit." Avoid holding the treat too high that the mutt has to jump for it. Rather, hold it in a position where he will have to stretch his neck. Immediately his rump hits the floor, tell him, "Good sit".

6. Repetitions tend to be crucial. However, your dog will get tired of multiple repetitions. To avoid that, play the sit game in short bursts several times throughout the day. Reinforce the sit command in other situations such as mealtimes.

7. Ask him to sit before putting his bowl of food on the floor, or before you open his door while taking him out for a walk. If he breaks the sit command, remind him with simple word like "oops. Try again".

The Come Command

Come command is one of the most useful tools for managing an annoying behavior in puppies. This command is used to help your dog get out of trouble or when giving him some work to do. You will use and refine this foundation skill for the rest of your dog's life.

How To Teach Come

1. Clip a light line on your dog's collar, then allow him to drag it around.

2. After he is familiar with the line, pick up one end and hold it as you follow him around. While he gets used to this, he will begin to realize that both of you are attached.

3. Keep the marker word in mind – "yes" – and a few treats, turn and walk backwards motivating him to follow along. After he twirls around and comes towards you, tell him "yes" with a treat.

4. Pair this behavior with the word "come". Each time he responds correctly, reward and praise him. Make this a game that he will enjoy playing.

5. Avoid yelling, "come, come, come, come," in case your dogs does not respond. Keep in mind that it is a one-word command and a one-word rule. However, when your dog understands the come command and after calling him he does not show up, you will have to gently guide him to where you want him to be.

6. When your dog is not responding to your command, it's either he does not understand or you are expecting too much from him.

Note: Never call your dog to come for discipline. If you do so, he will associate the come command with negative consequence. If you want to discipline your dog, go right to where he is instead of calling him.

The Stay Command

The stay command tends to be harder to learn for both young dogs and puppies. Asking a comfortably sited dog to move and stay somewhere else is almost asking for too much.

Just like any other command, the stay command is a lifesaver. A dog taught how to stay will never chase ducks in yards or charge at cows in the field. When your dog understands the stay command, he can participate in advanced obedience tricks or rally contests.

The stay command aims to teach a dog to remain still wherever he is until the further notice.

How to Teach Stay

1. Put a leash on your dog and sit comfortably next to him.
2. Waving a flat palm towards his muzzle, say, "stay".
3. Move in front of your dog for a few seconds, and then move back beside him.
4. Praise him for not breaking his stay.
5. In case he moves, calmly say "uh uh" or "oops" and take him back to the initial place. Again, give him the stay command together with the hand signal.
6. Practice this severally during the day in different locations

7. After you have rewarded him for the success, teach him words that will let him know when he is released from the stay. A nice release word is "okay".

The Down Command

The down command is an essential skill in managing your dog, keeping him out of trouble, and getting him out from underfoot. This skill tends to be a bit hard for some dogs because it is a submissive posture. A fearful or shy dog finds it hard to learn or perform the down command.

Note: It is very important that you go slowly while teaching your dog this skill and use lots of praise, and a happy, pleasant voice while teaching your dog this skill.

How to teach down

1. Hold a very pleasant treat in your hand and enclose it within your palm. Place this arm near your dog's muzzle.

2. After he notices the smell of the treat, start moving your hand towards the floor somewhere in front of him. His body will follow his head stretching out into a down. When he does, open your hand and give him the treat.

3. Repeat this several times daily and pair it with the word "down".

4. In case your dog lunges towards your hand, say "nope" and move your hand away before he gets to the treat. If he tries to sit up instead, break away and start again.

Note: Never try to push your dog into sitting down.

Encourage your dog for every bit of progress achieved until he completely understands the command. Often release him from the down and continue with other games.

The Walk Nicely On Leash Trick

A dog who does not pull or lunge at the end of his leash indicates he is a well-trained pet. A dog well trained to walk besides his owner is less likely to become fearful in new situations.

How to Teach Walk Nicely On Leash

1. Clip the leash to the buckle collar and using a happy voice to say, "let's go". Place treats in your bait bag or your left side pocket.

2. Encourage him to move forward by patting your left leg. Whenever he comes close to your side, pop a treat in his mouth.

3. After every few steps, stop praising him for being in the correct position.

4. If he lags behind or forges ahead, stop moving to let him wander to the end of his leash.

5. The slight tension on the leash will probably make him to turn around. Immediately after, you feel the leash slacken, utter the verbal praise word, "yes", followed by a treat and praise after he bounces back to you.

6. If he pulls, stop moving and he will auto correct his unwanted behavior. Then wait for him if he does not come back to your side.

Note: Loose-leash walking is best done if you are an active owner who is patient enough to teach his dog proper behavior even after making a hundred mistakes.

Once your dog starts walking on a loose leash, start to pair the behavior with the "heel" command that means, "stay close to my left leg whether we are walking or have stopped."

After you take a few steps with your dog in the heel position, praise and treat. Keep on practicing until your dog learns this command.

Note: Dog training is a continuous process; you just don't stop at teaching your dog basic commands. That's why you will need to advance your training to teach your dog a few advanced dog training commands to make you a cool dog owner. By teaching him or her some of the advanced commands, you will definitely feel more proud and cement your relationship with your dog. You can be sure that you will benefit a lot more from your best-friends-for-life relationship with your furry friend! Let's learn some of the advanced commands that you can teach your dog in the next chapter.

CHAPTER 5

Advanced Dog Training Commands

The Speak Command

Teaching your dog the speak command develops your dog's communication skills. The speak command teaches your dog to bark when he or she wants to get your attention. This is helpful because it helps your dog get used to the idea of speaking, which in this case means barking, whenever he needs to go outside.

You can also use the speak/bark signal to train your dog to alert you when there is a stranger nearby, when it is hungry, when its water bowl is empty, or when it wants to come back to the house.

How to Teach Speak/ Bark

1. Take a leash or a long line, and attach it to something secure such as a tree or fence.

2. Attach your dog by his wide buckle collar or a harness to the tie down.

3. Tie his toy on a short pole with a stick.

4. Dangle the toy back and forth in front of your dog making sure the toy remains out of reach.

5. Out of the frustration, your dog will bark at the toy.

6. When the dog barks, ensure to reward him by letting him or her to grab and even play with the toy for a short moment and then proceed to ask him to 'drop it'.

7. Continue doing this until the dog can bark regularly on command.

8. Add the 'bark command' and if the dog barks on command, offer some reward and positive reinforcement.

9. You can also teach your dog a hand signal once it has learnt to bark on command.

10. Show it the hand signal as you say the command.

11. After your dog masters the speak command as well as its adjacent hand signal, opt to use the hand signal instead of the verbal command.

The Quiet Command

One of the easiest ways to stop your dog from barking is to teach it the quiet command. You don't want your dog to start barking when you are in the middle of an important conversion or when you don't want to attract too much unnecessary attention. As long as you are in control of it, barking is a fine behavior in dog. It would be great to only let the dog to bark when you truly want it to bark as opposed to any other time.

How to Teach the Quiet Command

1. Encourage/wait for your dog to bark.

2. Allow your dog to bark a couple of times before showing it a tasty treat. Calmly utter the command word "quiet." Don't shout or be exited. Be calm and stay in control. When your dog catches the sight of the treat, it will focus its attention on it and stop barking.

3. If it remains quiet for 5-10 seconds, reward it.

4. If it starts barking before the 10 seconds, don't reward it.

5. Attempt the exercise again in a couple of minutes, this time rewarding it for remaining silent for 5 minutes.

The Wait Command

If your dog is highly energetic, you must teach it the wait command. The wait command tells your dog where he must stay until you let him know he can move. You can use this command in conjunction with the stay command but both are individual commands with different meanings to your dog.

How to Teach the Wait Command

1. Start by teaching your dog to wait patiently at the door. Place a leash on the dog and it ask it to sit.

2. Reach for the doorknob as soon as its rear touches the ground.

3. It will instantly get up. As it does so, pleasantly say 'Oops!' then take your hand away from the knob, and ask the dog to sit.

4. Reach for the doorknob again and the dogs makes to stand again, say 'oops' and take your hand away from the door.

5. Your dog will get the idea after a few trials. When the idea sinks in, challenge it by taking it outside.

How to Teach Wait Outside

1. Still on a leash, walk your dog near an obstacle such as a bridge, a flight of stairs, or the door.

2. Say the word 'wait' in a firm tone, as you move towards the obstacle while holding the leash taught.

3. If your dog stops and looks at you, praise it and give it a treat.

4. If it continues, give it a gentle tug on the leash and repeat the command. Say 'No, wait' in a more firm tone.

5. When your dog has successfully waited for a short time, let your dog know that it's ok to continue on by saying 'Ok.'

6. Repeat this exercise until the dog is responding immediately to the word 'wait.'

The Leave It Command

When your dog knows and understands the leave it command,

it will give you peace of mind knowing that you can effectively control the dog. How cool would it be when you don't have to worry about having to monitor your dog's every little movement even in an environment where there are nice treats?

How to Teach Leave It

1. Place your dog on leash, under control, and he cannot get to the object you are going to ask them to leave it. Choose something neutral that does not excite or bore your dog.

2. Place the item within the dog's sight; when he makes a grab for it, tell the dog to leave it; when the dog completes your command, click the training clicker, and give the dog a treat.

3. Repeat this 4-5 times.

4. Repeat the process with something your dog likes but does not love, and again, tell the dog to 'leave it.'

5. If the dog tries to take the object, pull back the object until it learns to ignore it.

6. Practice this exercise repeatedly until your dog willingly follows it command and ignores his favorite toy. Continue practicing with more challenging objects until the command sinks in.

7. Move your training outside where you can teach your dog to ignore other dogs, squirrels, and people. Click and reward every time your dog obeys.

The No Command

This command teaches your dog to stop doing what s/he is doing or s/he won't have something. You can use this command to stop the dog from engaging in unwanted behaviors such as jumping on you or someone else, chewing, or biting. This basic command will help you keep your dog well mannered.

How to Teach the 'No'

1. Teach this command when your dog is not full, but hungry enough to be attentive. Have several different kinds of treats that your dog really likes in your hand.

2. Hold one of those treats flat in your closed hand 6 inches from the dog's mouth.

3. Your dog will naturally try to grab it. Quickly say the word 'No!' in a firm tone, and quickly enclose the treat in your fisted hand.

4. If the dog fails to stop, simply pull your hand away from the dog until he resets and remains calm.

5. Place your open hand again at the dog's eye level about 6 inches from the mouth.

6. Once again, when the dog makes for the treat, quickly close your hands into a fist while saying 'No.' Repeat this process for 5 minutes then give it a five minutes break to reset the brain.

7. After 5-10 sessions, your dog will have grabbed the concept.

Note: Be quick to withdraw your hand. Your dog can be sneaky when it sees your hand open.

The Heel Command

The heel command helps you control your dog when on a walk, and when you are around other dogs or people. The heel command places your dog on your side instead of pulling on his leash.

It is a formal obedience exercise where your dog learns to walk by your knee, matching your pace and sitting down when you halt. This way, you will have better control of him should you meet another person or dog.

How to Teach Heel

1. Begin your lesson when your dog is in a calm frame of mind.
2. Place your dog on a leash. If this excites the dog, wait a few minutes until the dog calms down. Pick the leash up and begin to walk.
3. Offer your dog a treat to entice him to walk besides you, and offer it plenty of praises once your dog starts moving with you.
4. If it pulls on the leash and jumps ahead and starts pulling on the leash, stop and wait until it has stopped tugging and pulling.
5. Simply stand, patiently wait, and ignore your dog; do not yell or pull at the leash, simply hold a tautly.

6. Once your dog calms down, call him or her back and offer rewards, praise, and treats when he does as instructed.

7. Once you and your dog are moving together, say the word 'heel' repeatedly.

8. If your dog jumps ahead, stops, or lags behind, entice him or her back to your side, and begin again.

9. When your dog walks next to you when you utter the heel command, reward it with plenty of praises and an occasional treat.

10. Progressively practice this exercise in your home, then slowly extend the distance, switch the directions frequently, and remember to give your dog plenty of praises every time he or she follows the heel command.

The Stand Command

This command comes in handy at bath time or grooming time. It is a must teach command for any dog owner. So how do you make your dog to stand on command?

How to Teach Stand

1. Ask your dog to sit in front of you, about a foot away.

2. Hold a treat parallel to its nose, a few inches away and slowly move the treat forward towards you.

3. As your dog stands to reach for the treat, praise, and quickly give it the treat as a reward.

4. As it stands, offer the treat, use the stand signal, and praise your dog.

5. Practice this several times a day.

6. Once it is standing quickly with the hand signal, add the verbal cue "stand."

The Off Command

Even if you're comfortable with it, others might find it uncomfortable when your dog jumps on them. This command teaches your dog to stay down and not to jump up on you or anyone else. It also keeps your dog off the furniture.

How to Teach Off

1. Have your dog sit in front of you; in front of its nose, hold a treat the dog considers yummy. Don't allow your dog to grab the treat. Just let it sniff it.

2. As it paws at the treat and shows frustrations to get it, firmly give the verbal command 'Off!' without yelling.

3. As soon as it makes the slightest movement from your hand with its nose, give it the treat and praise it.

4. Practice the command using 5-15 seconds sessions several times a day.

The Jump Command

This command teaches your dog to jump in the air with all four paws off the ground, but not over objects. If you want to be the coolest dog owner in your neighborhood, this is definitely something that you want to teach your dog. There mere sight of your dog jumping on command will simply be amazing. So how do you teach your dog to jump on command?

How To Teach Jump

1. Get your dog exited.
2. Grab your touch stick and hold it closer to the ground so that your dog has to jump up to touch it.
3. Click, and treat your dog as soon as its legs are off the ground.
4. Raise the touch stick higher and let it jump again. Click and reward once it jumps.
5. Gradually push your touch stick higher and introduce the verbal word 'jump' every time it jumps. Keep praising and rewarding every time it jumps over.
6. Keep doing this until he eventually jumps at your command.
7. Stop using the touch stick and use your command instead. Click and treat whenever he does this.

The Drop Command

Your dog will use its mouth to pick up something that might be unhealthy/harmful for it. Dogs often swallow safety pins, needles, and other small objects before you can retrieve them.

The drop command will save you and your dog from the risk of injury. This command makes playing fetch more fun when your dog returns with ball and drops it at your feet or in your hand for another toss.

How to Teach Drop

1. Gather 3 items, a toy your dog likes, the one it loves, and some treats your dog likes.

2. Choose a quiet place free from interruptions

3. Give your dog a toy that it likes and allow it to play freely.

4. Give the 'drop it' command when you are ready. Say this command only once.

5. Then move the tasty treat slowly right in front of your dog's nose.

6. As soon as the dog drops the toy, ensure to praise and then treat it.

7. Repeat this exercise at least 5 times the first time you do it and a couple of times thereafter.

8. After about a week of practice, give your dog a toy they love instead of the one they like.

9. Repeat the same procedure replacing the toy with a treat. Before advancing the game again, revert to an item your dog likes less if he fails to drop the item.

10. Stop giving your dog a treat every time it follows through.

11. Continue repeating the exercise with progressively more challenging toys and treats. Every time something is in your dog's mouth is an opportunity to train the drop it command by asking the dog to 'drop it' and praising and treating him/her whenever they do it.

The Fetch Command

Playing fetch is a great way to have fun with your dog, and exercise him at the same time. A dog can be very particular about the toy it plays fetch with. Experimenting with different toys will help you determine which one it loves most. The instinct to retrieve is innate in your dog's genes. Fetching simply means go out, bring it back, and give it up.

How to Teach Fetch

1. Line up several toys and treats. Leave the food reward out of the picture.

2. Toss a toy your dog likes, a few feet away and point to it.

3. As it chases for the toy, encourage your dog to come back to you by reaching for the toy in his mouth and tugging on it. It will get the idea that bringing the toy back to you leads to a tugging battle. Eventually, you won't have to play tug every single time your dog fetches.

4. If your dog brings the toy back to you, shower it with praises but don't take the toy away.

5. If after getting the toy, your dog ignores you, pretend to eat some of its yummy treats.

6. Say 'bring' as your dog catches on and trots happily to you.

7. Toss a toy it likes most and go through the same procedure again.

Now that you are familiar with some of the advanced commands that you can teach your furry friend, you also want to learn a thing or two about making your dog social. We will learn all that in the next chapter.

CHAPTER 6

Socialization Skills

Socializing for your dog is very important especially when you want to ensure that your dog is comfortable and well behaved around other people and animals. It's recommended to socialize your dog while he is young and continue socializing him all through his life to maintain the social skills.

Remember that in socialization sessions, everything seems strange to your dog. In this case, introduce everything to him in a calm reassuring way so he can adjust to the new world. Keep the exposure short to avoid overwhelming your dog.

There are several ways of socializing your dog, starting from inviting people to your home, to enrolling your dog for socializing classes. Below are some ways to keep your dog socially active.

Expose Your Dog to New Experiences and People between the Ages of 3 -12 Weeks

Dogs at the age of 3-12 weeks are more accepting to new experiences. During this time, expose your dog to as many, new but safe places as possible, i.e. to other animals and pets, vehicles, humans of all ages and sizes, and everything about outdoor life. Your dog's checklist of the things he should be exposed to is as follows;

- Children- in case you don't have kids at your house, take your dog to a park where he can meet children playing (bearing in mind if the park allows you to bring your dog with you). Take time with your dog there, so he can see and listen to the kids as they play.

- Unfamiliar people of different sizes, gender, and ethnicities- expose your dog to every type of people as long as they are willing to handle him in a positive manner. Let him come across people wearing hats, boots, and jackets.

- Other pets/animals- in case you don't have another pet in your house, take your dog to a dog park where he can safely socialize with other dogs. You can as well expose your dog to your friend's cat or any other pet by just sitting calmly next to them.

Consider Enrolling Your Dog for Socialization Classes

Socialization skills are offered at veterinarian clinics, community centers, and large pet stores. These classes aim to introduce your dog to many new experiences and sights such as people, other dogs, puppies, various sounds, smells, sights, and equipment. Your dog will be allowed off its leash to play with different people and other dogs. This will help your dog get to know other dogs and people.

Basic obedience classes go along with socialization skill classes since the dog is exposed to sounds such as contraction sounds, traffic, odd sounds through the use of discs, and many other sounds.

CHAPTER 7

Training Dos and Don'ts

Training a dog can be difficult for the inexperienced. However, for the persistent, it is a rewarding experience. The following dog training dos and don'ts will help you avoid common pitfalls while training your dog.

Do Find a Distraction Free Location

Always teach your dog new commands at a location that is free from any form of distractions. This will enable your dog to focus on learning. After getting conversant with the command, you can slowly introduce distractions.

Don't Assume Rewarding Your Dog for Good Behavior

Many dog owners are accustomed to rewarding their dogs during training but forget to reward the dog for continued good behavior. It is crucial to reward your dog after following commands like "stay" and "drop it", to reinforce their importance. Also, don't keep on rewarding the dog to do basic commands; instead, you should make the rewards sporadic then phase them out after some time. In so doing, you will not need to carry treats all the time to get the dog to do stuff. For instance, don't be giving food treats all the times; you can offer a quick pat, a quick praise or anything else that you believe the dog loves but be quick to reward him if you have to.

Do Use both Verbal and Hand Cues

Loss of hearing and blindness are common afflictions for an older dog. Using both cues can retain the capability of communicating with your pet even after losing his sight or sense of hearing.

Don't Plan Sessions Longer Than 20 Minutes

It's unfair to expect a young dog to concentrate on learning for a period of more than 20 minutes. Rather, find only 20 minutes to work with your dog on a daily basis. After he reaches maturity, his attention span will develop allowing you to extend the sessions as you wish.

Do Practice Commands At Various Locations

Young dogs cannot comprehend that "sit" and "stay" commands are universal. According to the dog trainer website, a "stay" taught inside the house, has a slight connection to a "stay" practiced in a backyard. In this manner, practice your commands in different locations so your dog can associate the command with your hand signals and voice rather than location.

Don't Use An Excited Voice To Earn Your Dog's Attention

Using an excited voice will help you get your dog attention, but it's not recommended to compete with your dog for his attention. Use a firm and calm voice to give commands without repeating the cue. This will enable your dog to be coming to you even after he sees something else that is more exciting.

Do Reinforce Pack Behavior at All Times

Your dog should perceive you as the head of your house before you begin training. Don't do anything that portrays you as the weaker party in your relationship otherwise the dog will try to do anything he wants because to him, he is the pack leader. This means that you shouldn't be overly excited when you see him, or pamper him with lots of treats for stuff. To build that relationship, you will have to reinforce good behavior and constantly punish bad behavior. Ensuring that your dog is heeling while on a regular walk is one way of building that bond.

Don't Be Afraid To Take Your Dog to a Dog Trainer

Even though you have not enrolled for a standard 8-week obedience course, think of scheduling a few appointments with a dog trainer. A dog trainer will give you insight into your dog's mind making the training easier.

Do Stay Calm

Dog training needs a lot of positive reinforcements and patience. Don't yell at or hit your dog since you want loyalty and not fear. Also, don't repeat a command multiple times because this only teaches the dog that they will only have to respond after multiple repetitions. I know this can be hard but it has to be done otherwise you will have a hard time training the dog.

Don't Stop Until Progress Has Been Made

Many dog owners end up getting frustrated and stop training before their dogs learn to respond to commands. Dog trainers say this reinforces bad behavior in your dog making him think that acting up will get him out of training.

Do mind your body language

Dog's can easily decode your body language so be careful how you act around the dog when issuing different commands or instructions. You don't want the dog to misunderstand you. For instance, don't just hold the treats out in the open when telling the dog to something. You will need to hide some of the treats to make the training more exciting for the dog and the rewards more sporadic. Otherwise, the dog will see it as if they are being bribed to do something. You also don't want the dog to be too dependent on treats to follow commands. And if the treat is in the pocket, keep your hands out of the pocket to ensure the dog doesn't just associate your hands in the pocket with treats. Instead of associating the treat with the command, he will instead associate the treat with hands in the pocket and this is not what you are trying to teach. Make the dog keep guessing! In addition, ensure to treat the dog just about anywhere; don't have a specific place where you issue the treats otherwise that's the only place the dog will associate with treats. As such, move to different parts of the house and outside the house to give treats.

Do expand the number of commands you teach your dog

Learning is only exciting to a dog if you constantly teach him new stuff. Just like humans, once we have mastered something and can do it with ease, we get bored. This also applies to dogs. Dogs too can start getting bored with the same old routine. As such, you should train your dog new skills and commands to make your dog an all rounded canine friend who is just adorable for everyone who sees how the two of you relate. Some of the commands you can teach him include:

- Drop on recall
- Leave it
- Drop it
- Clicker training
- Retrieve over high jump
- Wait
- Heel
- Long sit down (5 minutes)
- Long sit (3 minutes)
- Focus
- Retrieve on flat
- Broad jump

- ✓ Stand for examination
- ✓ Heel free
- ✓ Long sit (1 minute)
- ✓ Go out
- ✓ Off the couch
- ✓ Sit on street corners

Conclusion

You have just learnt everything you need to train your dog. Always remember to reward your dog every time he does anything right. This is the most crucial part of the training. Treats keep your dog interested and helps cement your bond.

Bear in mind that some dogs are tricky to train and may need more training time. You need to exercise calmness and patience and never yell at your dog, as this will only cause problems in the end.

Puppy Training

The Complete Guide To Housebreak Your Puppy in Just 7 Days

Introduction

I want to thank you and congratulate you for purchasing the book, *"Puppy Training - The Complete Guide To Housebreak Your Puppy in Just 7 Days"*.

This book has actionable steps and strategies on how to housebreak a puppy in just a week.

Owning a puppy is an amazing thing, as a puppy brings an incredible feeling of immense joy. In as much as having a puppy is a great experience, there are also challenges that come with owning a puppy. One of these challenges is house training. There is nothing exciting about finding your puppy always peeing on your sofa, carpets and anywhere possible you can think of. Hence, with owning a puppy comes the responsibility of house breaking the puppy and ensuring that they don't urinate everywhere in the house but in a specific designated area.

The thought of housebreaking a dog often makes many new puppy owners feel highly nervous and worried because house breaking a puppy is not an easy job. A lot goes into ensuring your dog pays heed to your instructions and always excretes in the designated area instead of littering everywhere in, and outside the house.

If you intend to housebreak your puppy but haven't been able to achieve any success, this book is the perfect match. This book

Dan O'Brian

is a definitive guide to house training your dog in just seven days. Yes, you read it right, 7 days. Follow this guide and you'll successfully train your puppy in a week.

Thanks again for purchasing this book, I hope you enjoy it!

Table of Contents

Introduction 53

Understanding Your Puppy's Psychology 57

The Importance Of Crate Training In House Breaking 65

Day 1: Setting Your Puppy's Routine 67

Day 2: House Breaking A Puppy - A Few Don'ts,
And How To Avoid Them 73

Day 3: Poop Patrol- Identifying Your Dog's
Poop Signals 77

Day 4: Choosing The Right Training Method
For Your Puppy.. 79

Day 5: Condition Your Puppy - The Magic Of Positive
Reinforcement 87

Day 6: Using the Startle, But Never Scare Method 93

Day 7: Practice All That You Have Learned 95

Conclusion 97

MY 1st FREE GIFT TO YOU!... 99

My 2nd Free Gift To You! 101

Understanding Your Puppy's Psychology

Before embarking on housetraining your puppy in seven days, you must make some effort to understand your puppy's psychology and know him or her better. This will make it easier to train him, or her ☺.

Let' start by doing that

Understanding Your Puppy

As a puppy/dog owner, you must:

Realize That A Puppy Is Like A Little Baby: The first thing you must understand is this; your puppy is still a baby; you cannot expect it to grasp everything you are saying or commanding from day one. Sure, a puppy is capable of doing a lot more compared to a human baby at eight weeks, but that doesn't mean the puppy is all grown up.

You have brought him into your house, which is a comforting place for you, but an entirely new environment for him. At first, your puppy will feel strange and might not respond to you in an affectionate manner from day one. This is why you need to give the puppy time to adjust to the new environment.

Show love and care to your furry baby to make it feel welcomed and loved. This will help the puppy understand that you are a loving owner and think only what is best for it, which will end up making it easier for your puppy to follow your instructions.

Don't Delay the Process: Even though you should give your puppy about a week to settle into the new environment, you must not delay the housebreaking process. You may think it is best to train the dog when it grows older since it's only a baby now and you would have to give it a great amount of time. However sound this approach sounds, it is wrong.

Until he or she becomes 12 weeks old, puppies do not have control over the muscle that lets it hold pee; if you don't make haste to train your puppy to pee and poop outside, or in a set location in the house, it is going to defecate all over your house. Your rug will smell of pee, and your favorite reading spot will be soiled with poop, and the more a place smells like pee, the more the puppy will urinate here because they associate the area with pee.

Understand Mother Nature: Housebreaking a dog is relatively simple when you understand Mother Nature. Similar to how mothers' potty train children at a certain age, a dog also trains her kids to excrete outside, or next to their pen whenever she feels her pups need to excrete.

After birth, puppies normally eat and excrete inside the den. The mother notices this act and cleans all the mess to ensure the filthy odor does not remain on her pups, or in the den. As they grow, she starts nudging them to go outside the den to excrete. With time, they learn to excrete far from the den. This shows that it is in a dog's nature to excrete outside their place of residence. In your case, the only difference is that you will play the role of your puppy's mother; therefore, it is your duty to train him.

Know the Dog's Nature: Another important thing you must comprehend prior to starting the seven-day plan is your dog's nature. This entails two things: the breed and needs of your puppy, and the dog's nature to please the master.

Dog's Breed: Each dog is different and belongs to a specific breed. Every breed has its own set of needs and requirements, and behaves in a certain manner. Before beginning the housebreaking process, you must completely understand your dog; understand what he likes to eat, how much it eats, how many times it urinates and poops, how its digestive system works, and how long it takes him to excrete after a meal. This information will accordingly help you train your dog, and enable you to create a routine that suits both, you and your furry little friend.

Dogs Love to Please: The second thing you must bear in mind is that it is in every dog's nature to please the master. Dogs don't like it when you, the master, is upset; thus, a dog always wants to do things that please the master.

It is likely your puppy will exhibit the same behavior. It will become upset upon seeing you angry, and will run towards you and show signs of excitement when you smile at him. You must learn to make the best use of this in-built dog behavior and use it to your advantage.

Observe your dog closely to show resentment towards his poor behavior such as peeing inside the house, so he knows that this act has made you angry.

Accompany Your Puppy Everywhere: If you see him peeing on the rug, but take five to six minutes to show your disapproval, the puppy will think you are upset because of the mess on the floor and not the act of relieving himself on the rug. Therefore, he will continue with this practice and will become sad and confused upon seeing you infuriated, but won't understand the problem.

Ensure to accompany your dog everywhere during the first few days of its arrival in your home. Follow him wherever he goes, so you can promptly show your resentment if you find him excreting inside the house. This helps the pup understand the reason behind your resentment, which, with your guidance of course, helps him gradually eliminate this behavior to please you.

Let's swiftly move on to the next section.

Puppy Owner's Manual: Figuring Out If You're Ready Or Not

As much as it is important to understand your dog's psychology and determine the ideal time to train him, you also need to figure out whether or not you ready to venture into the housebreaking process.

As a dog owner, you're responsible for training your dog and make it follow rules so it never leaves puddles of urine and bundles of poop everywhere in your house. Therefore, it is imperative to get some insight into your routine, needs, and psychology as well, so you can begin this process at the right time.

How to Know If you're ready to start the House Training Process

As we indicated earlier, housetraining your puppy is not a walk in the park. It requires a lot of dedication, time, and commitment. In this regard, you must prepare yourself and ensure you're ready to embark on the training. How do you know, or how can you tell if you're ready? You're ready if:

You Have Sufficient Time: Housebreaking a little pup means following him wherever he moves. If he goes into the bathroom, you must follow it; if you find it sneaking into the kitchen, you need to run after it.

You need to be on your toes the entire time your puppy is moving around; this is important so you can examine the pups behavior, know when it excretes, and show it resentment promptly if it poops in the house. Therefore, housebreaking a puppy is a hectic job and one that demands you to invest a great amount of time. Therefore, you must begin this process when you have sufficient time at your disposal.

This doesn't mean you have to stop working, or take a seven day leave from the office. It merely means you must be ready to give proper time and care to your pup once you reach home from work; and if you don't work, then you must be prepared to invest a portion of time to training your dog.

If you have a big office presentation or project coming up, or have to prepare for your wedding, then it is best to postpone dog training for a few days and begin this process once you are through with the hectic and time-consuming jobs; this will allow you to focus entirely on puppy training once you get started.

Are Ready to Stay Alert and Active: The housebreaking process demands that you stay active and alert. This allows you to observe your dog and notice the different pee or poop indicators it portrays.

Prepare your mind and body to remain attentive and energetic once you start with this process. You don't need to increase your daily caffeine intake to stay alert 24/7 because too much caffeine is bad. However, you can drink herbal teas, such as ginseng and rhodiola rosea teas to stay energetic. Studies show that both these teas can help combat fatigue and improve your energy levels.

Are Ready To Calm Yourself And Remain Calm: Often, new dog owners experience nervousness when housebreaking a dog; they lose their calm when they see the dog peeing on their favorite couch and start shouting at the dog. This stresses the dog, often making it experience depression. To properly house train your dog, you need to remain calm and always stay in a relaxed, cool mood.

Sure, it infuriates you when your pup fails to understand a signal or follow your command. Irrespective of how much truth that statement holds, the right way to make a pup understand your displeasure is to show resentment via your expressions and not your voice. Before you begin training your dog to excrete in a designated area, spend some time training yourself to stay cool and calm with your furry friend. Tell yourself that this process isn't an easy one, but with time and patience, you'll definitely get there.

Be patient with your pup and give him your love and support so he or she can pick on the cues and commands easily, and follow them conveniently. To stay calm, practice deep breathing and resort to this practice every time you are angry with the puppy.

The Importance Of Crate Training In House Breaking

Before we can move on to learn about house breaking, it is important to look at crate training. Crate training is important since you need to find a permanent home for your puppy, which in this case would be the crate. Furthermore, since dogs don't usually like excreting where they sleep, crate training your dog will ensure that the puppy gets used to their crate as their home and does not defecate in their crate but will wait for you to take them to the designated area. So how exactly do you crate train your puppy? Let us find out.

How Crate Training Works

Get a Suitable Crate: You need to purchase a crate for your dog according to his size and breed.

Next, place the crate in an area that most of the family members spend their time. The dog needs to feel like they are still people around and they are not in some room alone.

Make the Crate Comfortable: Add a few elements of comfort such as some toys or a comfortable blanket in the crate. This provides a comforting, welcoming environment for your pup encouraging him to enter the crate. You can also use treats and different positive reinforcement strategies to lure your dog into the crate.

Drain Him Off the Extra Energy: Before making your dog enter the crate, try making him exercise a little. This drains him off all the extra energy; he becomes relaxed when he has to enter the crate and doesn't make any fuss inside it.

Get Your Puppy: Get your puppy to come close to the crate and enter it. Use words like "enter pup" or "go in" to encourage the puppy to move into the crate. Do not try to drag the puppy into the crate, as this will make them see their crate as a bad place to be. It is important that the puppy gets in the crate alone. The treats that you put into the crate will serve as a way of getting your puppy into the crate.

Once your puppy enters the crate, allow them to find comfort in the crate and just as he does, gently close the door and sit close to the crate so your dog can see you and feel like they are not alone. Do not allow the puppy to stay in the crate for too long. The first time, you can let them stay in the crate for 30 minutes then over time, you can increase this time until they are comfortable being in the crate.

The sections that follow will outline an easy, seven-day process guaranteed to housetrain your puppy_ or any dog for that matter.

Day 1: Setting Your Puppy's Routine

The last few sections have equipped you with an understanding of the basics of housebreaking your puppy; at this point, you're ready to begin the process.

The first day of the seven-day training and house breaking plan focuses on making efforts to set your dog's routine. Why is setting a routine for your dog the first thing you must do?

Importance Of Setting A Routine

When you set a proper routine for your puppy, you will ascertain that your dog eats at certain times, and excretes at specific times. Although there will be days when your pup will bring variations to your time, and will change his eating or pooping schedule a bit, the routine will more or less remain the same. This makes things easy for you because you will know when to direct your pup to move towards the excreting area, or go outside.

Moreover, setting your dog's routine makes life simple and easy for him. He gets his meals on time, and excretes accordingly. This will help his digestive system work smoothly and efficiently and experience less problems. Secondly, a routine will help your pup sleep on time every night and wake up fresh the next morning.

Pups who haven't become accustomed to pooping and urinating routinely often wake up several times from their sleep and wake up grumpy the next day. To ensure you, your family and puppy stay healthy and happy; your first priority needs to be setting a daily routine for your little friend.

Here's how you can accomplish this goal.

How To Set Your Pup's Routine

Setting a routine for your dog isn't difficult; it simply requires a little patience and care. The guidelines below will help you set a routine for your puppy.

Wake Your Pup at a Specific Time

The first thing to do when setting your pup's routine is to wake the pup at the same time daily. Ensure that this time is after you wake up daily so he does not wake up before you do and soil your room. If you wake up at around 8, make sure to wake your puppy at around 9. Right after you wake it up, give it a warm hug, and then take it to the specific area where it pees.

Walk the Dog

Once your puppy is fresh and awake, let it walk outside. Make sure not to carry it because it will make your pup accustomed to this habit and he would want you to pick him up and take him out every time. Start walking in front of your pup and ask it to follow you. Once your dog is outside, let it excrete in a certain area.

Feed Your Dog

After your puppy has finished excreting, let him accompany you inside and give it breakfast. It is essential to feed your pup at this time every single day. Give him a sufficient amount of the meal in the bowl and make sure to take it away once he is finished eating.

If your pup finds the bowl in the eating-place, or in their den, they are likely to eat from it every now and then. This would disturb their eating regimen, making them excrete repeatedly. Therefore, it is essential to feed your pup a specific amount of food at specific times of the day to ensure it does not excrete repeatedly.

Make sure your pup Naps Daily

Ensure your pup naps for an hour or two daily to ensure it's eating and excretion times remain aligned and consistent.

Set a Play Time

Setting a specific playtime is essential to your pup's wellbeing; it allows the pup to get a break from the monotonous routine, feel fresh and happy, and enjoy living with you.

Play with your pup for about one hour. This helps the two of you bond, bringing you and your pup closer, which makes it easier for him to consider you the master. The better bonded you and your pup are, the easier it will be for your pup to follow your instructions regarding housebreaking.

Schedule Consistent Excretion Times

Schedule consistent pooping and peeing times for your pup. To set excretion times for your pup, you must understand the pup's anatomy.

A dog excretes about four times daily, which makes it a bit difficult to train the pup in a few minutes. Therefore, when you let him out to poop or pee, give him sufficient time to do it.

A puppy normally defecates about five to thirty minutes after eating a meal. Keep this information in mind when setting the right excretion time for your pup. After properly feeding your puppy, make sure to take it out in the open after five to six minutes. Give the puppy forty minutes to wander around the 'elimination spot' so he can relax and defecate easily. Soon, this practice will start serving as a trigger for your pup, making it excrete easily. Make sure to take your dog to the exact same spot for defecating each time. This is important because your puppy starts becoming familiar to certain scents, places and areas, and when you take your pup to the same spot at a certain time frequently, it will know it needs to excrete. Keep these guidelines in mind and take your pup out three to four times a day to relieve according to its food intake.

Set a Sleep Time

Lastly, focus on setting sleep time for your pup so it sleeps at the same time daily and gets a good night's sleep and wakes up fresh and active the next morning.

Keep this procedure in mind and practice it with your dog on the first day to set its proper routine. This technique does not end on this day. You must continue with this routine for the remaining six days.

Day 2: House Breaking A Puppy - A Few Don'ts, And How To Avoid Them

The first day taught you how to create a routine for your puppy so you can get him accustomed to the routine and let him know that he has to poop or pee at a specific time and at a designated area and not wherever he wants.

On the second day, you are going to reinforce learnings from the first day, and are going to focus on understanding some essential don'ts of housebreaking a dog.

Housetraining A Pup: Don'ts

There are certain do's of housebreaking a dog, such as setting up its routine and practicing positive reinforcement. Similarly, there are certain don'ts of this process as well.

These don'ts are there to help you understand things you must not do when potty training your dog. Avoiding these don'ts will ensure you train your dog the right way and don't upset him or her, or condition the dog to negative elements.

Below are things you **MUST NOT DO** when housetraining your pup:

Changing their Food Brand

When potty training, never change the brand of your dog's food, as sudden changes in the diet can upset your doggy's tummy, give the puppy diarrhea, and change the pup's excretion routine and timings.

Additionally, don't offer your dog any table scraps as it can fill his tummy too much, making it poop more than his usual routine.

Free Feeding

Free feeding is never a good idea, since it gives your dog the chance to eat as much as it wants and then poop as much as it wants and that too, at unpredictable times. This upsets the routine you worked so hard to create on day one.

Physical Punishment

If you find your dog excreting somewhere other than the set location, you must not throw any object at it, even if it is something soft as a wool ball. Punishment is not an effective method of training. Instead of encouraging your dog to follow the routine, it confuses your dog because it now thinks that they should not defecate and this can lead to greater health problems.

Dual Housebreaking

Decide whether to indoor train your dog, or outdoor housebreak them. Dual housebreaking is a big **'No No'**; it confuses the dog and often leads to stress. Pitts, a popular dog trainer based in California always advises his clients to practice either one of the two: outdoor or indoor elimination and then stick to that (more on these methods in later chapters).

Rubbing His Nose in Poop or Pee

According to various dog-training experts and the American Humane Association, rubbing a dog's nose in its mess is an abuse, and an unacceptable behavior. Your dog does not comprehend why you are doing this, and may start fearing and avoiding you.

Leaving Your Pup Unattended for a Long While

We have already established the need to be around your pup all the time when you are housebreaking it; do not leave your pup unattended. If you have to do something urgent while the pup is out in the open, run that errand fast, and return to your pup quickly.

Withholding Water from your Thirsty Dog

If you find your dog panting for water, give him the drink he needs. Never withhold water from your thirsty pup as a way of making him pee less, since just as you need water to survive, so does your dog.

On the second day, keep all these points in mind and avoid exercising them as you train your puppy. If you find yourself doing any of these actions, stop the moment you realize your mistake and take a few deep breaths. It is human to err but to train your dog correctly, ensure not to continue with these don'ts.

Day 3: Poop Patrol- Identifying Your Dog's Poop Signals

Well done! You are through with the first two days of the plan and that's a noteworthy achievement. On this day, you are going to practice an effective technique that will help you easily understand the excretion timings of your puppy.

Just like humans, dogs practice certain gestures and make some moves that signal that they want to excrete. You must learn how to look for, and identify such signs in your dog to understand him better and to know when he needs to relieve himself.

A three to four week pup won't be able to give any visible signs when he wants to pee because he cannot hold his pee; but a bigger pup will mostly give one or all of the following poop and pee signals. So, watch out for them.

Restlessness

Most dogs tend to become restless when they want to excrete. They start moving here and there, begin circling a certain spot and might even grasp hold of an object and tug it hard. If you observe these signs in your dog, then it is likely he wants to poop or pee.

Sniffing

Dogs become used to the smell of their toilet area after a few days and have the habit of sniffing it when they are eliminating.

Therefore, if you find your dog incessantly sniffing the floor or anything else, it is probable they are telling you to take them out to their toilet spot, so they can defecate.

Door Scratching

Some dogs start scratching the door, or even bark at it when they want to go out to the toilet. If you see your dog doing the same, take it out so it can excrete and become calm.

Whine

Certain dogs start whining softly and then gradually increase their whine intensity when they want to relieve themselves. If you know your dog is well fed and isn't stressed out, but find him whining nonetheless, then it is likely that he wants to visit his toilet.

Poop and pee signals vary from one dog to another, but most dogs practice the aforementioned signals. You need to study your dog very closely and observe how he behaves just when he needs to excrete, so you can understand his toilet signal and pay heed to that sign promptly.

Day 4: Choosing The Right Training Method For Your Puppy

On the fourth day, you are going to decide on one housetraining method for your pup and then stick to it. As stated earlier, there are two main housetraining methods: indoors or outdoors.

The indoor method has two tributary types. This chapter will she some light on the different housebreaking methods, along with the factors you need to consider when choosing a certain method, which will allow you to select the most appropriate method for your dog.

Indoors Vs. Outdoors Housebreaking: Which One Should You Use

Indoor housebreaking involves training your dog to excrete at a fixed spot inside the house. You use newspapers, or a litter pan to ensure your dog relieves him or herself at a particular indoors spot (we shall discuss these three methods in a while.)

Outdoor housetraining involves teaching and training your pup to defecate outdoors. You can use newspapers, litter pans etc for outdoor training, but generally, these tools are not a necessity in outdoor housebreaking.

Opt for outdoor housetraining if your dog is:

Large and excretes enormous piles and puddles, can easily use the doggie door, you can assist him or her get to the potty area outdoors and if there is an open area outside your house that is suitable for use for defecating.

However, if your pup is small and excretes small piles and puddles of poop and pee, or you have a hectic work schedule and cannot guide her outdoors regularly, or there isn't an appropriate potty area outside your house, or you want her to be trained indoors, then it is best to choose the indoor housebreaking method.

Using these tips, you can easily decide which of the two plans suit you and your puppy best. Let us discuss these plans individually.

Outdoor Housetraining

To begin outdoor housetraining, first choose a suitable area outdoors where your dog can pee and poop comfortably. Opt for an area with a big patch of soil. There must not be any wild plants, especially ones with thorns; also opt for a wide, open area.

Next, begin training your dog using the outdoor housetraining steps listed below:

Choose a Phrase that Tells Him to Go Excrete

You could select anything, such as 'go pee', 'go potty', 'go empty yourself', or anything else. Your dog will grow accustomed to these words and will soon follow their command. You can also use newspapers or a litter pan to make your dog excrete at a certain spot outdoors, but these tools seldom find use in the outdoors housebreaking method.

Figure Out Your Pup's Defecation Time

Next, figure out your dog's pee and poop time. You have been working on developing his routine, right. This is where that will come in handy. As you have most likely created your dog's routine, you can easily determine when your dog needs to excrete.

Often, dogs excrete when they wake up, after drinking or eating, and once during playtime. Once you have figured out your dog's excretion time, use the phrase you created earlier to command him to go out and pee.

To ensure your dog follows your command and goes outside to excrete, you could use the umbilical cord method, or dog door.

Let's look closely at these techniques.

The Umbilical Cord Method

The Umbilical cord method refers to keeping your dog attached to you all the time as a fetus attaches to its mother via an umbilical cord. In your case, a leash is going to act as the umbilical cord. Get a leash and attach it to your pup's collar. Fasten the leash to its pen or any other object whenever you don't want to hold it, and unfasten it to take hold of it when you want to take your dog outside to poop or pee.

When you're aware that your puppy needs to relieve himself, hold his leash and take him outside. Make sure, you make him walk. This method is suitable for you if you have sufficient time at your disposal and can spend that time with your dog, and if your dog likes being leashed. If your dog is not yet comfortable with the leash after a few days, then it is clear it doesn't like this method of training; you should instead try using the dog door.

Using the Dog Door

Some dog owners find it easy to use a dog door for housetraining their dogs. You can use the same tool if it suits you. Get a dog door relative to the size of your dog, and install it in your door.

Next, make your dog walk through the dog door whenever you find him signaling that he wants to excrete. During the first two to three days, you need to open the flap of the door yourself to ensure the flap doesn't hit and scare your puppy. In about two to three days, your pup will grow accustomed to this tool and will use it successfully. This method is suitable if you want your dog to become independent.

Let Your Pup Poop

Next, you need to let your pup go out and take time to relieve himself. Don't utter any word or give him a signal that shows he must hurry through the process. This will make him hold some of the pee inside, which will upset the routine.

Keep practicing this routine for the remaining four days and by the end of the seven days, your will have housetrained your pup. You must remember to use positive reinforcements when your puppy obeys a command and follows the routine properly (we'll look at positive reinforcement in subsequent chapters).

Indoor Housetraining

Indoor house training is most suitable for puppy owners who may live in apartments and don't necessarily have a backyard that the dog can use. The common indoor housetraining method is paper training. Let us look closely at this method.

Paper Training

Paper training is a popular indoor housetraining method wherein you use old newspapers to help your dog excrete in a fixed spot. In this method, you place a pile of old newspapers in any spot you wish for your puppy to use as an excretion point.

You must use the same spot each time to ensure your dog becomes used to excreting on paper and at a certain spot, and stops going to a different prohibited place each time. Moreover, paper absorbs feces and urine, making it easier for you to clean up, as you simply need to take the soiled paper and discard it. This method is extremely easy, simple, and cheap. You can also use puppy pads or litter pans for this method.

Litter pan training is the same as paper training, except that in litter pan training, you use a litter pan instead of newspapers to serve as your dog's toilet. Litter pans are available in supermarkets and stores that sell housebreaking tools and supplies.

How to Paper Train your Dog

This method is best for you if you don't want to spend extra on getting a pan for your pup and want a disposable technique. So how do you go about paper training your puppy?

Choosing a Spot

To begin paper-training your dog, decide on a spot that will serve as your pup's toilet. It is best to choose a small room or area you can confine using a puppy gate. Choose an area that has linoleum, tiled, or hardwood floor because these floors are easy to clean and don't soak up any urine.

Never opt for a carpeted area because the carpet will absorb the urine making it difficult to get rid of the annoying urine odor. Secondly, your pup will start enjoying the softness of the carpet and will want to poop on it instead of the paper. A spot in the laundry room, bathroom, or just outside the kitchen usually works well.

Covering the Area with Paper

Next, cover the entire room with puppy pads or newspaper. Set your dog's bed, a few of its favorite toys, and a water bowl at one nook of the room. Next, bring your puppy to this spot.

Let Your Puppy Take its Time

After your puppy is in the toilet area, let them take their time to excrete. Make sure to remove paper near where the puppy sleeps. Puppies have a natural instinct to avoid soiling their sleeping area. Therefore, if you remove paper from close to the bed, the puppy will avoid excreting in that area. Watch your pup closely and ensure it eliminates on the paper only. Every day, tear off some of the paper covering the room, so that you restrict your pup to defecate in one particular spot only. By the time you reach the seventh day, your pup would have perfected this technique.

Now that you know all the best and commonly employed dog training methods, you need to select one on the third day and start exercising it so you can train your dog to practice the method easily.

Positive reinforcement, encouragement, and conditioning will help you motivate your furry friend to obediently follow your instructions and make a proper habit of excreting in the designated spot. Let us discuss these methods in the next chapter.

Day 5: Condition Your Puppy - The Magic Of Positive Reinforcement

You have selected, and started with a housetraining method. Now you need to ensure that your puppy obeys you and pays heed to all your commands, so he sticks to the method you chose.

To ascertain that, condition your dog to eliminate in the toilet area. To accomplish this goal successfully, you need the help of positive reinforcement.

Understanding Positive Reinforcement

Can you recall how your parents conditioned you to work hard at school? By giving you a few dollars or buying you a gift every time you got good results or by appreciating your effort, they showered their love on you in different forms whenever you did something good and that encouraged you to continue with that behavior.

This is what positive reinforcement is and exactly what you need to exercise with your pup. Positive reinforcement makes your furry baby obedient and makes practicing the housetraining methods we discussed earlier easier.

But you must adhere to the guidelines below so you employ the strategy the right way.

Correct Timing

Just as you must time when you show resentment towards your puppy when he does something wrong, you as well need to be very accurate with positive reinforcement.

You must reward your pup as soon as he practices good behavior. For instance, if you see him walking out the dog door as per your instructions, immediately reward or praise him. To ascertain that, observe your dog all the time.

Keep the Commands Short

Dogs cannot understand long sentences. Therefore, make sure to keep the commands short and clear when instructing them. For instance, avoid saying, "Billie, I want you to go poop in the litter pan." Instead, you should say things like, "watch me, stay, come, follow, sit, stand, off, leave it, go, poop" and similar short commands.

Be Consistent

Consistency is the key to positively reinforcing your dog to behave obediently and practice housetraining successfully. This is why you need to ask all family members to use similar commands, so your puppy does not become confused. In addition, everyone should be rewarding and unrewarding the exact desired and undesirable behavior, respectively.

When To Positively Reinforce Your Pup

Positively reinforce your doggie with treats and appreciation when she follows you to her toilet, and excretes properly, follows you back inside, eliminates on the right spot every time and goes in and out of the crate without creating any fuss.

Of course, you must use positive reinforcement when he or she performs any other good behavior; but here, our focus is primarily on housetraining. Make sure to avoid using positive reinforcement to shape bad behavior.

For instance, if you let your dog outside as a reward for being compliant with the housebreaking rules, don't let him out if he misbehaves. Your dog won't consider that as a punishment and will perceive it as a reward. Therefore, be careful when choosing reward and giving the reward to your dog.

Kinds Of Rewards

There're a variety of rewards you can use to condition your dog to practice good behavior and practices. These include, giving food treats to your pup, petting the pup, giving the pup a toy she loves, or indulging the puppy in his or her favorite game.

Note: Choose a treat or reward that entices your pet.

Your pet must not be able to resist that treat. An enticing treat will motivate your pup to continue obeying you in order to get the treat in return. Secondly, the treat needs to be small so your dog can instantly gulp and eat it. Don't give your dog a big biscuit or a bone because your dog will have to chew it, which will create a mess on the floor.

Also, avoid using meals as a treat. There needs to be a difference between a treat and a regular meal. In addition, keep a number of different small treats handy to ensure your dog stays involved in this practice and does not become bored of one particular treat.

In addition, appreciate your dog every time he follows a housetraining guideline successfully besides giving him the treat. Dogs love words of appreciation. Therefore, make sure to verbally praise your furry friend, try different rewards on your dog to find out which ones work best and only carry a few of the most effective ones.

Continuous And Intermittent Reinforcement

In the beginning, you should reward your pup each time he practices a certain potty training rule properly. This practice is referred to as 'continuous reinforcement;" it stimulates your pet to carry on with the good behavior. Once, your pup reliably and successfully learns a behavior, you need to switch from continuous to intermittent reinforcement wherein you continue with the reward, but gradually reduce its frequency.

In the first five to six days, you should reward your puppy with a treat each time he exercises a certain good housetraining behavior. After five days, reward her three of five times. Carry on with this for a few days and then reward her two of five times. Keep cutting back after every few days until you reward her occasionally. Intermittent reinforcement helps shape good behavior in your pup without making the pup greedy for treats.

Praise your dog each time he follows your command, but your appreciation can become less effusive than before. For instance, if you used to show extreme excitement and say lots of nice things to your puppy when she used to poop in the designated area, after a week, you should resort to 'good dog' only. However, you should show great excitement occasionally too so your puppy knows you are not angry.

Practice everything we have learnt in this chapter so you can correctly condition your pup to your chosen potty training method. Positive reinforcement will make your pup extremely obedient, so you won't have to worry about your entire house getting filthy with his piles and puddles.

Day 6: Using the Startle, But Never Scare Method

On the sixth day, practice startling your dog when he misses an instruction or breaches a housetraining rule. Mostly, when you see someone going against your wishes or breaking a regulation, you tend to scare them with a shout or your loud tone.

It is likely that you will do the same with your pup when you see her pooping on the kitchen floor and not the newspaper. This act of scaring your dog is wrong and is likely to upset him instead of disciplining him.

On the sixth day, attempt to eliminate this behavior; instead, opt for the startle method.

How To Use The Startle, But Never Scare Method

Startling your dog means to make him or her attentive towards you to help the pup understand that whatever he or she is doing isn't right. If you see him peeing on the floor instead of the designated area, clap loudly instead of chanting his name loudly. The clap will startle him and make him aware of the wrong behavior. You could choose any startling gesture such as a snap of the fingers or a knock on the door. Make sure to stick to that gesture and practice it every time you find your dog disobeying you.

Be Consistent

Ask all household members to practice similar commands and rewards, and ask them to exercise the same startling gesture as well. If you clap at your dog when he pees at a different spot each time, then everyone else should clap at this behavior too. This helps your dog become conditioned to that gesture and understand that whatever she is doing is unacceptable.

Make Your Pup Practice the Right Action

After you have startled your pup, make him carry out the right practice and then reward him. This helps the pup know what he or she is supposed to do and the reward works as an incentive to make him continue with the good behavior.

Day 7: Practice All That You Have Learned

On the seventh day, carry on with all that you have learned in the past six days. You have decided on a potty training method, know your pup's routine, know what signals to look out for, and are aware of positive reinforcement, and how to use it; use these techniques to ensure your dog sticks to its schedule, and the selected housebreaking method. The seventh day is going to be easy for you because your dog will have grown accustomed to this regimen and would easily obey your commands.

By simply exercising the steps in this guide, you can train your dog to follow your instructions, defecate in the right are, help keep your house neat and clean, and keep himself tidy at the same time.

Conclusion

With the help of this guide, housetraining your puppy becomes incredibly simple. By following the effectual and beneficial techniques and methods we have outlined here, you can easily train your pup to pee and poop in the right spot every time; this will keep your house immaculate.

Implement this guide and experience amazing results in a mere seven days. Good luck. ☺

MY 1st FREE GIFT TO YOU!

As a way of saying thank you for purchasing my book, I'd like to send you an exclusive gift that will help with using Dogs potty training.

Dog Potty Training is a quick and exclusive guide on how to potty training your dog in 11 steps. Check it out and bring the best version of yourself out NOW!

I am giving you this FREE BONUS to thank you for being such an awesome reader and to make sure I give you all the value that you deserve!

Dan O'Brian

To get your FREE gift, type in the URL below and follow the steps & I'll send it to your e-mail address right away.

https://maikon.leadpages.co/puppy-potty-training-/

My 2nd Free Gift To You!

As a way of saying thank you for purchasing my book, I'd like to send you an exclusive gift that will help with your dog training skills. It will also help with training your dog.

100 Dog Training Tips is 100 quick and exclusive tips to transform your dog even more. Check it out and bring the best version of your dog out NOW!

I am giving you this FREE BONUS to thank you for being such an awesome reader and to make sure I give you all the value that I can in your mission to have a Happy, Obedient, Well Train Dog!

To get your FREE gift, type in the URL below and follow the steps & I'll send it to your e-mail address right away

http://www.dogtrainingkindlebook.com/

Thank you again for purchasing this book!

I hope this book was able to help you to housebreak your puppy.

The next step is to implement what you have learnt.

Finally, if you enjoyed these books, would you be kind enough to leave a review for the books on Amazon?

Thank you and good luck!

Made in the USA
San Bernardino, CA
21 June 2016